Marketing Calculations

Market – Price –Profitability
Advertising

Calculations with detailed answers
Business Culture – Case Studies

Claude LAVEINE

Certaines informations de ce livre sont purement anecdotiques et imaginaires. Toute ressemblance avec une personne physique ou morale existante ou ayant existé est purement fortuite.

This book is a work of fiction. Any resemblance to a natural or legal person, existing or having existed is purely coincidental. The anecdotes and information cited are the fruit of the author's imagination.

Copyright©2020 Claude LAVEINE
Tous droits réservés.
ISBN-13 :9798552163281

From the same author

La Vie Epatante de l'Agent Secret Duchemin – Tome 1
Il Faut Sauver l'Agent Secret Duchemin – Tome 2
Agent Secret Duchemin – Mission Lune – Tome 3
Au Temps en Emporte l'Agent Duchemin – Tome 4
Le Fabuleux Destin de l'Agent Duchemin – Tome 5
Agent Secret Duchemin – En Avant Mars – Tome 6
Agent Secret Duchemin – A Mars Forcée – Tome 7

L'Effarante Aventure de Brian Tabernak – Tome 1
L'Incroyable Attaque de l'Agent Tabernak – Tome 2
La Terrible Traque de l'Equipe Tabernak – Tome 3
L'Equipe Tabernak Contre-Attaque – Tome 4
Des Agents pas très Secrets – Opération Esturgeon
Des Agents pas très Secrets – Mission Caméléon

Constantin Dumoulin – Panique sous les Tropiques
Constantin Dumoulin – Branle-Bas de Combat aux USA
Constantin Dumoulin – Secret Fatal au Lac Baïkal

Robin Dubois – Sans Froid ni Loi
Robin Dubois – Espion malgré moi

The Exciting Life of Secret Agent Duchemin – Volume 1
The Amazing Adventure of Brian Tabernak – Volume 1
The Incredible Attack of Agent Tabernak – Volume 2

Quiz de Marketing – Tome 1
Quiz de Marketing – Tome
Quiz de Marketing International
Quiz de Management Commercial
Comment s'autopublier en une journée ?
Marketing Quiz

Table des matières

From the same author 4

- Marketing Calculations - 8

Market Study 10

2. Break Even Point 33

3. Psychological Price 49

4. Advertising 60

5. Sales Management 83

Business Culture 118

International Negotiation 130

- Case Studies - 142

From the same author 147

- Marketing Calculations -

This book is aimed at Marketing, Business and Organisational Behavior teachers and at all the students learning Marketing Techniques in Business and Management Schools.

All the exercises are corrected with detailed answers to help the teachers and students to understand how to calculate and conclude.

The calculations are dispatched among several themes :

1. Market Study,

2. Break Even Point,

3. Psychological Price,

4. Advertising,

5. Sales Management.

In order to prepare the students to Business life, many Business Culture questions are listed and corrected after the calculations.

For helping teachers or students to think about Marketing Strategy, some Case Studies are proposed at the end of the book. These Case Studies can be prepared in teamwork.

Market Study

A company cannot launch a product/service without a market study. The marketing concept is to sell products/services our consumers want to buy. We can create a product/service and then try to sell it, but frequently it will be difficult to find buyers.

Because of hard competition, in a free market, we have to use the marketing techniques.
If we want to find customers, we need to ask them : what do you want to buy and why ?

Most of the time, a market study is based on interviews with test customers.
We ask them many questions about the competition, the market and their feelings.

Most of them are selected at random or because they represent an accurate type of customer.
We also need to analyse the main figures of our market, the turnover estimate, the potential expenditures, the budget.

Net Bank – Chelmsford (U.S.A)

Mr CREDIT, your managing director would like to increase the deposits amounts on saving accounts. You have to help him for this task.

	Number of Households	Annual Income (current year)	Total Income
Craftsmen - Shopkeepers			
Professional persons – senior executives			
Middle managers			
Employees			
Farmers - skilled workers			

A the end of the current year, the Net Bank 1,863 customers have invested $ 46m on saving accounts.
The Net Bank objective for next year is $ 26,000 per saving account, can you reach this goal ?

. Number of households in the county : 24,000.

Domestic American figures :
. Craftsmen – shopkeepers :
15 % (average annual income : $ 45,000)
. Professional persons – senior executives :
15 % ($ 84,500)
. Middle managers :
20 % ($ 38,000)
. Employees :
20 % ($ 20,000)
. Farmers – skilled workers :
30 % ($ 23,000)

. Next year, their annual income should increase by 1.5 %
. The county wealth index amounts to 0.8
. Additional revenues (pensions, allowances) : 15 % of the total annual income
. Amounts saved by households : 5 % of their total income
. Penetration rate planned by Net Bank – Chelmsford : 12 %

1/ Total income for the current year :
2/ Total income increased by 1.5 % for next year :
3/ Total income (for next year) according to the county wealth index :
4/ Total local income plus additional revenues :
5/ Amounts saved by households :
6/ According to the penetration rate of Net Bank – Chelmsford, amount collected :
7/ Saving account amount for next year :
Conclusion :

Answers

Net Bank – Chelmsford (U.S.A)

1/ Total income for the current year :

	Number of households	Annual Income (current year)	Total Income
Craftsmen - Shopkeepers	3,600	X 45,000 :	162,000,000
Professional persons – senior executives	3,600	84,500	304,200,000
Middle managers	4,800	38,000	182,400,000
Employees	4,800	20,000	96,000,000
Farmers - skilled workers	7,200	23,000	165,600,000
			910,200,000

2/ Total income increased by 1.5 % for next year : 923,853,000 (Q.1 + 1.5 %),
3/ Total income (for next year) according to the county wealth index : 739,082,400 (Q.2 x 0,8),
4/ Total local income plus additional revenues : 849,944,760 (Q.3 + 15 %),
5/ Amounts saved by households : 42,497,238 (Q.4 x 5%),
6/ According to the penetration rate of Net Bank – Chelmsford, amount collected : 5,099,668.56 (Q.5 x 12%).
7/ Saving account amount for next year : $ 46m + 5,099,668.56 / 1,863 customers = 27,428 which is above the objective : $ 26,000.
. Conclusion : The saving account goal is achieved. The result is satisfactory.

Organic World - Nashua (U.S.A – Mass)

As a local Manager of a new organic products store in Nashua (Massachussetts), you need to determine the potential yearly revenue of your local shop.
Your business area is divided into three districts.

	County #1	County #2	County #3
Number of inhabitants	980	396	1,944
Number of persons per household	2	1.5	2
Local consumption index	103	95	114
Attraction rate	96%	78%	57%

In Massachussetts, the average spendings per household for organic products amount to $ 275 per year.
Your local shop should attract 35 % of the local organic market.
For each county, you need to calculate the number of households, the number of attracted households, the local spendings for organic products, the total revenue.
Then you will have to add the three results and keep 35 % of the total.

Answers

Organic World - Nashua (U.S.A – Mass)

Number of households :
490 (County 1 ; 980 / 2)	264 (Cty 2)	972 (Cty 3)

Number of attracted households :
470 (Cty 1 ; 490 x 96 %)	206 (C.2)	554 (C.3)

Local spendings :
283.25 (C.1 ; 275 x 1.03)	261.25	313.5

Total revenue ($) :
133,127.5 (470 x 283,25)	53,817.5	173,679

360,624 x 35% = $ 126,218 (Potential yearly revenue)

AMC – TV Channel (U.S.A)

As a sales manager at AMC, you are in charge of promoting the Pay Per View Combo. You have to prepare the sales budget for next year. The yearly Pay Per View Combo subscription (including 45 hours of free PPV programs, free internet and discount phone calls) is sold $ 500.

According to the sales forecasts, and owing to the company knowledge, the formula used is :
Y = 200 T + 3000
T is the number of the Quarter (for the first Quarter, T = 1).

Seasonal coefficients :
. Quarter One :   0.8
. Quarter Two :   0.7
. Quarter Three :   1.2
. Quarter Four :   1.4

Sales executives objectives :
Mr A : 25 % ; Mr B : 30 % ; Mr C : 45 %

Monthtly fixed wage : $ 10,000 ; Variable commissions : 8 % of the total turnover.
What will be the budget amount for this sales team ?

1/ Sales Forecast :
. Quarter 1 :
. Quarter 2 :
. Quarter 3 :
. Quarter 4 :
. Total :

2/ Sales objectives per salesman :

	Q.1	Q.2	Q.3	Q.4	Total
Mr A					
Mr B					
Mr C					
Total					

3/ Sales team costs :

	Q.1	Q.2	Q.3	Q.4	Total
Fixed wage					
Mr A					
Mr B					
Mr C					
Total					

Answers

AMC – TV Channel (U.S.A)

1/ <u>Sales Forecast</u> :
   Quarter 1 : 500 ((200 x 1) + 3,000) 0,8 = 1,280,000
   Quarter 2 : 500 ((200 x 2) + 3,000) 0,7 = 1,190,000
   Quarter 3 : 500 ((200 x 3) + 3,000) 1,2 = 2,160,000
   Quarter 4 : 500 ((200 x 4) + 3,000) 1,4 = 2,660,000
   Total : 7,290,000

2/ Sales objectives per salesman :

	Q.1	Q.2	Q.3	Q.4	Total
Mr A	320,000	297,500	540,000	665,000	1,822,500
Mr B	384,000	357,000	648,000	798,000	2,187,000
Mr C	576,000	535,500	972,000	1,197,000	3,280,500
Total	1,280,000	1,190,000	2,160,000	2,660,000	7,290,000

3/ Sales team costs :

	Q.1	Q.2	Q.3	Q.4	Total
Fixed wage	90,000	90,000	90,000	90,000	360,000
Mr A	25,600	23,800	43,200	53,200	145,800
Mr B	30,720	28,560	51,840	63,840	174,960
Mr C	46,080	42,840	77,760	95,760	262,440
Total	192,400	185,200	262,800	302,800	943,200

The budget amount for this sales team is $ 943,200

KingRent – Roisssy CDG

As an assistant Manager for the KingRent rental unit located in Roissy CDG, you are interested in assessing the store indicators, compared to the shop site competitors.

A few criteria have been selected. When the following table is filled, analyse KingRent performance regarding its competitors results.

	KingRent Year NR-1	KingRent Year NR	C. X NR-1	C. X NR	C. Y NR-1	C.Y NR	C. Z NR-1	C.Z NR	Total NR-1	Total NR
Number of rental vehicles	87	87	47	47	72	72	46	46	252	252
Number of rental days	23,632	23,838	11,969	11,633	21,143	20,944	12,005	12,638	68,749	69,055
Average price	€ 52.20	53.86	48.84	53.62	49.01	54.75	48.85	51.27	50.05	53.62
Number of available vehicles			17,155	17,155					91,980	91,980
Rental rate			69.77	67.81					74.74	75.07
Availability share			18.65	18.65					100	100
Market share			17.41	16.85					100	100
Performance			Ms 1.24	Ms 1.80						

Ms = minus
C. = Competitor

. **Number of available vehicles** = number of vehicles x 365 days

. **Rental rate** = (number of rental days / number of available vehicles) x 100

. **Availability share** = (number of rental vehicles / total number of rental vehicles) x 100

. **Market share** = (number of rental days / total number of rental days) x 100

. **Performance** = Market share – Availability share

2/ According to these figures, which competitors appear to be the most dangerous for our KingRent rental unit in Roissy CDG ?

Answers

KingRent – Roisssy CDG

As an assistant Manager for the KingRent rental unit located in Roissy CDG, you are interested in assessing the store indicators, compared to the shop site competitors. A few criteria have been selected. When the following table is filled, analyse KingRent performance regarding its competitors results.

	KingRent Year NR-1	KingRent Year NR	C. X NR-1	C. X NR	C. Y NR-1	C.Y NR	C. Z NR-1	C.Z NR	Total NR-1	Total NR
Number of rental vehicles	87	87	47	47	72	72	46	46	252	252
Number of rental days	23,632	23,838	11,969	11,633	21,143	20,944	12,005	12,638	68,749	69,055
Average price	€ 52.20	53.86	48.84	53.62	49.01	54.75	48.85	51.27	50.05	53.62
Number of available vehicles	31,755	31,755	17,155	17,155	26,280	26,280	16,790	16,790	91,980	91,980
Rental rate	74.42	75.07	69.77	67.81	80.45	79.70	71.5	75.27	74.74	75.07
Availability share	34.52	34.52	18.65	18.65	28.57	28.57	18.25	18.25	100	100
Market share	34.37	34.52	17.41	16.85	30.75	30.33	17.46	18.3	100	100
Performance	- 0.15	0	Ms 1.24	Ms 1.80	2.18	1.76	- 0.79	0.05	-	-

Ms = minus
C. = Competitor

31,755 = 87 x 365 ; 74.42 % = 23,632/31,755 x 100 ;
34.52 % = 87/52 x 100 ;
34.37 % = 23,632/68,749 x 100 ; - 0.15 = 34.37 - 34.52

. **Number of available vehicles** = number of vehicles x 365 days

. **Rental rate** = (number of rental days / number of available vehicles) x 100

. **Availability share** = (number of rental vehicles / total number of rental vehicles) x 100

. **Market share** = (number of rental days / total number of rental days) x 100

. **Performance** = Market share - Availability share

2/ According to these figures, which competitors appear to be the most dangerous for our KingRent rental unit in Roissy CDG ?

The most dangerous competitor is C.Y, despite a high price increase it maintained its market share and a good performance. That means they use a customer service strategy : yield management (prices) and probably a loyalty card together with a high level of motivation for the front desk.

2. Break Even Point

The break even point can be determined in volume (products sold) and in turnover ($, €).
Especially for a new company, it is essential to estimate this break even point. We need to know when we are able to cover our full costs (Variable and Fixed costs).

The first cent of profit will be essential for the company. At the break even point, we have no profit, no loss.
A company cannot survive without any profit. We need to innovate, to create new product/services and to recruit new employees and executives.

On average, we lose almost 10 % of our customers each year, for multiple reasons. Some of our products/services decline because of new technologies and new competitors.
The break even point helps us to determine the B.E.P date and the volume/turnover estimate.
These figures are necessary to prepare a budget, to plan the sales objectives and the commissions of the salespeople.
Il will also help the company in planning the costs.

The variable costs depend on the turnover, the more we sell, the more we must pay our salespeople (commissions, bonuses).

The fixed costs do not change, whatever the turnover. Even if we do not sell anything, we must pay the office rental, electricity, heating.

Big Buy – U.S.A

Big Buy is very interested in launching new Vending Machines which would operate 24 hours.

These B.B Vending machines will be located as a market test in most of the Universities and Colleges of New England.

Each vending machine will propose at least 140 products including food, beverages, stationery, hygiene and cosmetic products.

This new kind of service is very appreciated by students and BigBuy will develop this new concept with franchisees.

As a new franchisee of B.B Vending machines, you want to analyse the profitability of one machine which would be installed at Upton College.

"BigBuy" sent you the following figures :

. Cost of goods sold : $ 720,000
. Franchisor royalties :   5 % of the annual revenue
. Advertising royalties :   5 % of the annual revenue
. Building rental : $ 5,500 per month
. Yearly costs :
. Insurances : $ 10,000
. Electricity * : $ 40,000
. Supplies* : $ 2,000
. Staff and Social contributions* : $ 400,000
. Depreciation : $ 50,000
. Taxes* : $ 30,000
. Financial expenses : $ 40,000

*60 % are variables costs.

. Expected annual revenue : $ 2m

1/ Fill the following Costs classification and Income statement tables.
2/ What might be the annual turnover to break even ?
3/ How many products should be sold to break even (average selling price : $ 9) ?
4/ At what date should you break even ?

. Breakeven turnover =
Turnover x Fixed costs / Contribution Margin
. Breakeven volume =
Breakeven turnover / selling price
. Breakeven date =
(Breakeven turnover / Turnover) x 360 days

Costs Classification

	Fixed Costs	Variable Costs
Yearly rental		
Insurances		
Franchisor royalties		
Advertising royalties		
Electricity		
Supplies		
Staff and Social contributions		
Depreciation		
Taxes		
Financial expenses		
Total		

Income Statement

	Amount	%
Annual turnover		
Cost of goods sold		
Variable costs		
Total Variable costs		
Contribution margin		
Fixed costs		
Net income		

. Total variable costs =
Cost of goods sold + Variable costs
. Contribution margin =
Turnover – Total variable costs
. Net income =
Contribution margin – Fixed costs
. Each % is obtained by dividing each element by the turnover and multiplied by 100

Answers

Big Buy – U.S.A

Costs Classification

	Fixed Costs	Variable Costs
Yearly rental	66,000	
Insurances	10,000	
Franchisor royalties 2 m x 5%		100,000
Advertising royalties 2 m x 5%		100,000
Electricity	16,000	24,000
Supplies	800	1,200
Staff and Social contributions	160,000	240,000
Depreciation	50,000	
Taxes	12,000	18,000
Financial expenses	40,000	
Total	354,800	483,200

2/ 2,000,000 x 354,800 / 796,800 =
890,562 (Breakeven turnover)
3/ 890,562 / 9 = 98,951.3 products to break even, or 98,952.

Income Statement

	Amount	%
Annual turnover	2,000,000	100
Cost of goods sold	720,000	
Variable costs	483,200	
Total Variable costs	1,203,200	60.18 %
Contribution margin	796,800	39.84 %
Fixed costs	354,800	17.74 %
Net income	442,000	22.1 %

. Total variable costs = Cost of goods sold + Variable costs
. Contribution margin = Turnover – Total variable costs
. Net income = Contribution margin – Fixed costs
. Each % is obtained by dividing each element by the turnover and multiplied by 100

4/ 890,562 / 2,000,000 x 360 = 160.30 days. 160 / 30 days = 5.33 months.
0.33 x 30 days = 10 days. 5 months plus 10 days = June 10th.

GoodFun Resort – Orlando – USA

In order to convince new customers in the Orlando area, GoodFun Resort's Marketing department decided to propose a new yearly Passport, including a free access to the two amusement parks (GoodFun/GoodFun Studios) together with 3 free nights at the Wild West Ranch.
The unit selling price of this new Pass will amount to $ 200.
For this special promotion, the following costs have been determined.

1/ Fill in this "Costs classification table" :

($)	Total expenses	% of Variable costs	% of Fixed costs	Variable costs amount	Fixed costs amount
Advertising costs	1,200,500	100		1,200,500	0
Overhead expenses	245,500	70	30	171,850	73,650
Taxes	45,200	40	60	18,080	27,120
Social contributions	112,800	60	40	67,680	45,120
External expenses	5,500	50	50	2,750	2,750
External database	80,500		100	0	80,500
Financial expenses	38,400		100	0	38,400

. Total Variable costs : 1,460,860
. Total Fixed costs : 267,540

2/ Fill in the following Income statement :

(€)	Amount	%
Annual Turnover	2,125,000	100
Variable costs		
Contribution margin		
Fixed costs		
Net income		

. Contribution margin = Annual turnover − Variable costs
. Net income = Contribution margin − Fixed costs

3/ What might be the turnover and volume of Pass sold to break even ?

4/ At which date would it be possible to break even ?

5/ What should be the annual turnover if the net income amounted to € 500,000 ?

. Breakeven turnover = Fixed costs x Annual turnover / Contribution margin
. Breakeven volume = Breakeven turnover / Selling price
. Breakeven date = (Breakeven turnover / Annual turnover) x 360 days
. Contribution margin = Fixed costs + Net income

Answers

GoodFun Resort – Orlando – USA

1/ Fill in this "Costs classification table" :

($)	Total expenses	% of Variable costs	% of Fixed costs	Variable costs amount	Fixed costs amount
Advertising costs	1,200,500	100		1,200,500	
Overhead expenses	245,500	70	30	171,850	73,650
Taxes	45,200	40	60	18,080	27,120
Social contributions	112,800	60	40	67,680	45,120
External expenses	5,500	50	50	2,750	2,750
External database	80,500		100		80,500
Financial expenses	38,400		100		38,400

. Total Variable costs : 1,460,860
. Total Fixed costs : 267,540

2/ Fill in the following Income statement :

(€)	Amount	%
Annual Turnover	2,125,000	100
Variable costs	1,460,860	
Contribution margin	664,140	31.25
Fixed costs	267,540	
Net income	396,600	18.66

. Contribution margin = Annual turnover – Variable costs
. Net income = Contribution margin – Fixed costs

3/ Breakeven turnover :
2,125,000 x 267,540 / 664,140 = € 856,028
267,240 / 31.25 % = € 856,128

856,028 / € 200 = 4281 passeports must be sold to break even.

4/ 856,028 / 2,125,000 x 360 = 145 days / 30 =
4.83 months.
0.83 x 30 = 25 days. 4 months plus 25 days = May 25th.

5/   Contribution margin = 267,540 + 500,000 = 767,540
(Contribution Margin) 664,140 leads to (Turnover) 2,125,000
767,540 leads to X ?
664,140 x X = 2,125,000 x 767,540 so X = 2,455,841.

3. Psychological Price

The main issue for a company is to find the right price, for the right product/service at the right time. First of all, we must take into account our total costs in order to keep a minimum profit margin. This profit margin will enable to launch new products/services, to invest in the workforce, to innovate and to increase our turnover.

Most of the time we can sell at a higher price, at a lower price or at the same price than our competitors. Therefore, we have to analyse their pricing strategy and try to adapt to the market.
At the end of the process, we may use a Psychological Price study by interviewing test consumers regarding their feeling of the product/service.

According to their knowledge of the market and the competitors, they will give their opinion about the quality of the product/service and about the final price.
These exercises are able to give an estimate of the right price, according to the customers knowledge.

The final price, after all our market studies (total costs, competitors price, psychological price), will be a magical price. Always a few cents under the full price.
For example, 9,99 cents.

Surprisingly, whatever the product/service and the country, even one cent under the full price will enable to sell more than the full price, 10 cents. One of the mysteries of marketing.
Finally, the psychological price is a good summary of the marketing concept, how to adapt to the consumers and sell at the price they are looking for. And not the contrary.

Trans World Express – Roissy CDG

After a market survey in the Paris area, Trans World Express wants to propose a new service for small packages – a monthly subscription including a cell phone and internet alerts to confirm that the delivery arrived on time, whatever the number of packages sent each month. In order to sell correctly this new service, a consumer panel including 400 people has been interviewed regarding the price quality related. Two questions have been asked to this panel :

"Which price would be too high for this new service ?"
"At which price would you think this service would be of unsufficient quality ?"

Their answers are listed below :

	Answers "Excessive Price"	Answers "Unsufficient Quality"
Less than € 4	0	80
4 to 6	0	180
6 to 8	32	100
8 to 10	40	24
10 to 12	64	12
12 to 14	100	4
14 to 16	144	0
16 to 18	18	0
18 to 20	2	0
More than 20	0	0

1/ Fill in the following table in order to determine the psychological price.

2/ Propose a "magical" price for this new service.

% of Answers "Excessive price"	% of Answers "Unsufficient quality"	Added % Excessive price	Added % Unsufficient quality	% of Expected customers	Expected turnover
0		0		0	0
0		0		20	80 to 120
8		8		57	342 to 456
		18			
			4		
	1		1		
	0		0		
	0		0		
	0		0		
	0		0		

Expected customers = 100 − (column 3 + column 4)

Answers

Trans World Express – Roissy CDG

% of Answers "Excessive price"	% of Answers "Unsufficient quality"	Added % Excessive price	Added % Unsufficient quality	% of Expected customers	Expected turnover
0	20	0	100	0	0
0	45	0	80	20	80 to 120
8	25	8	35	57	342 to 456
10	6	18	10	72	576 to 720
16	3	34	4	62	620 to 744
25	1	59	1	40	480 to 560
36	0	95	0	5	70 to 80
4.5	0	99.5	0	0.5	8 to 9
0.5	0	100	0	0	0
0	0	-	0	0	0

Expected customers = 100 – (column 3 + column 4) ;
8 = 32 / 400 x 100 ; 18 = 8 + 10 ;
4 = 1 + 3 ; 80 = 4 x 20 ; 120 = 6 x 20 ; Psychological price = between 8 to 10 ;
Magical price = € 9.90

Boulangerie PIERRE – Paris

A new service will be proposed in Paris by Boulangerie PIERRE an early breakfast delivered at home from 5.30 A.M to 9.30 A.M. Boulangerie PIERRE would like to determine the psychological price of this new service, except from the food price. According to the following table (400 customers interviewed),

	Answers "Excessive Price"	Answers "Unsufficient Quality"
3	0	168
6	0	135
9	0	58
12	2	20
15	15	11
18	33	7
21	40	1
24	66	0
27	95	0
More than 30	149	0

Fill in this table in order to determine the psychological price and then a "magical price":

% of Answers "Excessive price"	% of Answers "Unsufficient quality"	Added % Excessive price	Added % Unsufficient quality	% of Expected customers	Expected turnover
0		0		0	0
0		0		42	252
0		0		75.75	
0.5		0.5			
		4.25			
			2		
	0.25		0.25		
	0		0		
	0		0		
	0		0		

Answers

Boulangerie PIERRE – Paris

Fill in this table in order to determine the psychological price and then a "magical price" :

% of Answers "Excessive price"	% of Answers "Unsufficient quality"	Added % Excessive price	Added % Unsufficient quality	% of Expected customers	Expected turnover
0	42	0	100	0	0
0	33.75	0	58	42	252
0	14.5	0	24.25	75.75	681.75
0.5	5	0.5	9.75	89.75	1,077
3.75	2.75	4.25	4.75	91	1,365
8.25	1.75	12.5	2	85.5	1,539
10	0.25	22.5	0.25	77.25	1,622.25
16.5	0	39	0	61	1,464
23.75	0	62.75	0	37.25	1,005.75
37.25	0	100	0	0	0

$0.5 = 2 / 400 \times 100$; $42 = 168 / 400 \times 100$; $4.25 = 0.5 + 3.75$; $2 = 0.25 + 1.75$;

$42 = 100 - (0 + 58)$; $252 = 42 \times 6$.

Psychological price = € 15 ; Magical price = € 14.90

Even if the highest turnover is at € 21. Additional information would be needed : total costs, selling price of competitors.

4. Advertising

Advertising is an essential activity in Marketing. However many consumers think that they are saturated with advertising messages. Many people do not watch T.V channels anymore mainly because they are fed up with advertising. The recent success of streaming T.V channels and video on demand is the answer of disappointed consumers.

Advertising prices are always higher and represent a big amount of money for a company.
If we decide to advertise on the internet or in classical media, we must be sure of the final target and audience.

According to the very high costs of advertising, we have to select correctly the final reader, watcher or listener of the ad.

We must also be sure that we have an advertising budget and a correct media plan.
Our product/service must be seen or watched in the right media at the right time.
Some companies do not spend any money in advertising and use only word of mouth advices or social media. It can be efficient too.

WorldNet.com – France

In order to create customers loyalty, WorldNet.com decided to promote a loyalty card in France aimed at men over 40 years old. If the card testing is successful, this service will be extended to all other targets.

For this advertising campaign, 5 magazines have been selected.

For choosing the best media you need to calculate the following ratios :
. Target audience, Cost per thousand, Target ratio.
. Target audience = Total audience x Targets %
. Cost per thousand =
(advertising cost / target audience) x 1,000
. Audience ratio : (Target audience / Total audience) x 100

	Total Audience	% of Men	% of Men over 40 years old	Advertising cost*
Magazine A	1,000,000	75	20	€ 50,000
B	2,000,000	50	30	60,000
C	500,000	80	80	45,000
D	750,000	66.7	90	30,000
E	1,500,000	47	60	70,000

*full colour page

1/ Fill in the following table :

	Target audience	Cost per thousand	Audience Ratio
Magazine A	150,000	€ 333.33 per 1,000	15%
B			
C			
D			
E			

2/ Which media should be selected ?

Answers

WorldNet.com – France

	Total Audience	% of Men	% of Men over 40 years old	Advertising cost*
Magazine A	1,000,000	75	20	€ 50,000
B	2,000,000	50	30	60,000
C	500,000	80	80	45,000
D	750,000	66.7	90	30,000
E	1,500,000	47	60	70,000

*full colour page

1/ Fill in the following table :

	Target audience	Cost per thousand	Audience Ratio
Magazine A	150,000	€ 333.33 per 1,000	15%
B	300,000	200	15%
C	320,000	140,62	64%
D	450,225	66,63	60%
E	423,000	165,48	28%

150,000 = 1,000,000 x 75% x 20%
333,33 per 1,000 = 50,000 / 150,000 x 1,000
15% = 150,000 / 1,000,000 x 100

2/ Which media should be selected ?

Magazine D must be selected : highest target audience, cheapest cost per 1,000 contacts, almost highest percentage of audience ratio.

CoffeeStar – Paris

With a view to improving its customer service, CoffeeStar would like to propose a "drive through" service in its French restaurants.

It would enable many French customers living in the Paris area to buy their coffee and a breakfast directly from their car.

Very successful in the United States, this service will be promoted with an advertising mail for a testing store in the Paris suburbs.

First, a yearly subscription for large companies will be sold, including a "drive through" full breakfast 144 days per year (i.e : 3 days per week, 48 weeks per year).

According to the following figures, what might be the profitability of this direct marketing campaign ?

. Subscription selling price : € 1,847

. Cost of goods sold : € 990

. Advertising mail creation and printing :

. 5,000 copies : € 32,500   - 10,000 copies : € 55,000
 15,000 copies : € 70,000   - 20,000 copies : € 90,000
 (Leaflet weight : 28 grams)

. Usual achievement rate : 0.8 % (signed subscriptions)

. Stamping : 20 to 50 grams : € 2.08 (as from 1,000 mails) - € 1.79 (as from 15,000 mails).

. Calculate the profitability of this advertising campaign for the following number of mails : 5,000 - 10,000 - 15,000 - 20,000.

1/ For 5, 000 mails : Costs =
             Profit margin =
             Profitability (Profit margin – Costs) =

Answers

CoffeeStar – Paris

1/ *For 5, 000 mails* :
Costs = 32,500 + (2,08 x 5,000) = 42,900
Profit margin = 40 *(5,000 x 0,8%)* x 857 *(1,847 - 990)*
= 34,280
Profitability (Profit margin – Costs) = 34,280 – 42,900
= - 8,620 (Loss)

2/ *For 10,000 mails* :
Costs = 55,000 + 20,800 = 75,800
P.M = 80 x 857 = 68,560
Py = 68,560 – 75,800 = - 7,240 (Loss)

3/ *For 15,000 mails* :
Costs = 70,000 = 26,850 = 96,850
P.M = 120 x 857 = 102,840
Py = 5,990 (Profit)

4/ *For 20,000 mails* :
Costs = 90,000 + 35,800 = 125,800
P.M = 160 x 857 = 137,120
Py = 11,320 (Profit)

At least, 15,000 mails must be sent to make a profit during this direct marketing campaign.

Realtors 22 – Marne-la-Vallée

A new Realtors 22 store will open in the Marne-la-Vallée area, a local advertising campaign must be quantified. In order to promote this real estate service, a € 12,500 advertising budget is planned.
According to the following advertising costs and the media plan, calculate the total cost of the local advertising campaign.

. 100 thirty seconds advertising spots on the local FM Radio,
. 3 publications of a half page in the local Newspaper,
. An advertising leaflet (less than 30 grams) distributed in the shop site.

. <u>Local FM Radio</u> :
. *Price per unit for one 30 seconds spot* :
 < 100 :   € 42.70
 100 to 199 : € 41.16
 200 to 299 : € 38.11
 > 300 :   € 33.50

 . Advertising message creation : € 122
 . Technical expenses : € 11.50 per broadcasted spot

. <u>Local Newspaper</u> :
 . *For one publication* :
 One page : € 1,327, one half page : € 732, one third page : € 550, one fourth page : € 412

. *For three publications* :
One page : € 3,782, one half page : € 2,086, one third page : € 1,564, one fourth page : € 1,173

. Technical expenses : € 230

. <u>Advertising leaflet</u> :
< 100,000 leaflets distributed :
 < 35 g : € 33.39 per 1,000 - 35 to 70 g : € 39.18 per 1,000 - 70 to 150 g : € 45.12 per 1,000

> 100,000 leaflets distributed :
 < 35 g : € 31.71 per 1,000 – 35 to 70 g : € 37.35 per 1,000 - 70 to 150 g : € 42.84 per 1,000

. Leaflet creation : € 230
. Leaflet printing : € 0.125 per unit
. Number of shop site households : 10,752

. Fill in the following media plan :

	Cost per unit	Quantity	Total cost
Local FM radio :			
Message broadcasting			
Message creation			
Technical expenses			
Subtotal 1 :			
Local Newspaper :			
Message publication			
Technical expenses			
Subtotal 2 :			
Leaflet :			
Leaflet distribution			
Leaflet creation			
Leaflet printing			
Subtotal 3 :			
	Total advertising budget :		

Answers

Realtors 22 – Marne-la-Vallée

	Cost per unit	Quantity	Total cost
Local FM radio :			
Message broadcasting	41.16	100	4,116
Message creation	122	1	122
Technical expenses	11.5	100	1,150
Subtotal 1 :			5,388
Local Newspaper :	(for 3 publications)		
Message publication	2,086	1	2,086
Technical expenses	230	1	230
Subtotal 2 :			2,316
Leaflet :			
Leaflet distribution	33,39	10,752	359.01
Leaflet creation	230	1	230
Leaflet printing	0.125	10,752	1,344
Subtotal 3 :			1,933.01
		Total advertising budget :	**9,637.01**

(33.39 / 1,000 = 0,03339 per unit x 10,752)

It is a satisfactory budget as it is much lower than the objective of 12,500.

HolidayClub – Paris

HolidayClub would be interested in proposing a new travel insurance to its customers. "Easy travel" would cover all the risks during a trip : plane cancellations, delays, lost luggage, credit cards frauds.

In order to promote this new service, you can use two marketing techniques : advertising mail and phone calls. Your objective is to contact 200 customers with each technique.

1/ What would be the total cost of each operation ?
2/ Would you organise these two operations successively ?
3/ How long do you need to break even, for each operation ?

. **Advertising mail** :
. Stamping :   € 0.5 per mail
. Copies :   € 0.15 per mail
. Envelopes :   € 0.03 per mail
. Mail creation :   5 hours
. Routing :   27 seconds per mail
. Subscription rate : 10 %

. **Phone calls** :
. Phone communications : € 0.1 per minute
. Successful calls (with a subscription) :   18 minutes
. Demonstrated calls (with no subscription) :   6 minutes
. Short calls (no answer or failure) :   1 minute
. Subscription rates :
  . Successful calls :   10 %
  . Demonstrated calls :   35 %
  . Short calls :   55 %

This new service would be sold € 3 per month, with a 20 % profit margin.

Manpower cost : € 8.75 per hour, plus 60 % of social contributions.

Answers

HolidayClub – Paris

. **Advertising mail** :
Stamping + copies + envelopes = (0.5 + 0.15 + 0.03) x 200 = 136
Creation = (5 x 8.75) x 1.6 = 70
Routing = 27 seconds x 200 = 90 minutes (5,400 / 60) = 1.5 hour ; (1.5 x 8.75) x 1.6 = 21
Total = 227

. **Phone calls** :
200 contacts if done separately, or 180 contacts if done successively.
Successful calls : (200 x 10%) 20 x 18 mn x 0.1 = 36
Demonstrated calls : (200 x 35%) 70 x 6mn x 0.1 = 42
Short calls : (200 x 55%) 110 x 1mn x 0.1 = 11
Subtotal = 89
Manpower : (20 x 18mn) + (70 x 6mn) + (110 x 1mn) = 890 mn ; (890/60) x 8.75 x 1.6 = 207.67
Total : 296.67.

2/ Yes, advertising mail : 200 x 10% = 20 subscriptions, Phone calls : 180 x 10 % = 18 subscriptions.
Total = 38 subscriptions.

3/ Monthly profit margin (per unit) = 3 x 20% = 0.6 ; for 20 subscriptions, 0.6 x 20 = € 12 per month.
Advertising mail : (227/12) = 18.9 months to breakeven,
Phone calls : (296.67/10.8) = 27.46 months to breakeven.
10.8 = 0.6 x 18

These two operations can be organised separately (mail or calls) or successively (mail and calls).

5. Sales Management

Sales management is one of the most difficult tasks of a company. Even an excellent product/service will be hard to sell without salespeople. These salespeople are more and more difficult to recruit. Most of the Business Schools students dream of marketing jobs and do not want to sell anything. Surprisingly, marketing is first of all the art of selling, but for many people it is associated to strategy and advertising.

It would be strange to become a brand manager without a selling experience first.
Therefore, the salespeople need to be very well motivated. All the commissions and bonuses have already been invented and must be calculated correctly.

But, maybe the most important, salespeople need to feel good in the company.
Selling everyday is a hard job with many disappointing moments.

The sales objectives are more and more ambitious and the competitors are always more agressive.
That is why we need to calculate very precisely the motivation plans, the sales budget, the sales unit and salespeople efficiency.

HBM – New England (U.S.A)

As a manager at HBM (Cell Phone distributor) in New England, you have to dispatch the total sales objective : $ 233,000, according to the different targets and States.

Turnover in year Nr minus 1

$	Total Turnover	Small Accounts	Medium Accounts	Large Accounts	Public Cies	Crafts men
Massachussetts	54,238	3,700	3,463	27,120	7,950	12,005
Vermont	23,549	2,549	5,000	9,420	3,620	2,960
Maine	49,752	841	12,450	20,750	10,007	5,704
New Hampshire	51,874	8,372	6,720	15,562	12,720	8,500
Total	179,413	15,462	27,633	72,852	34,297	29,169

1/ Fill in this table :

	Turnover rate per target	Sales goal per target
Small Accounts		
Medium Accounts		
Large Accounts		
Public companies		
Craftsmen		

2/ Sales goal per target and State (in proportion) in year Nr :

$	Total Turnover	Small Accounts	Medium Accounts	Large Accounts	Public Cies	Crafts men
Massachussetts						
Vermont						
Maine						
New Hampshire						
Total						

Answers

HBM – New England (U.S.A)

As a manager at HBM (Cell Phone distributor) in New England, you have to dispatch the total sales objective : $ 233,000, according to the different targets and States.

Turnover in year Nr minus 1

	Turnover rate per target	Sales goal per target
Small Accounts	8.61%	20,061.3
Medium Accounts	15.4%	35,882
Large Accounts	40.6%	94,598
Public companies	19.11%	44,526
Craftsmen	16.2%	37,746

(15,462 / 179,413 x 100) = 8,61%
233,000 x 8.61% = 20,061.3

2/ Sales goal per target and State (in proportion) in year Nr :

$	Total Turnover	Small Accounts	Medium Accounts	Large Accounts	Public Cies	Crafts men
Massachussetts	70,368.54	4800.52	4,496.77	35,215.19	10,321.06	15,535
Vermont	30,561.53	3,307.1	6,492.59	12,231.82	4,699.65	3,830.37
Maine	64,574.24	1,091.1	16,166.57	26,943.78	12,991.56	7,381.23
New Hampshire	67,308.41	10,862.1	8,726.05	20,207.18	16,513.7	10,999.38
Total	232,812	20,060.1	35,881.98	94,597.97	44,525.97	37,745.98

$3{,}700 / 15{,}462 \times 20{,}061 = 4{,}800.52$

T.V + - Paris

As a Sales Manager of T.V + in Paris, you have to assess your sales representatives performance.

They are in charge of selling T.V + subscriptions to Hotels, Restaurants and Cafés in the Paris Area.

According to the following ratio, you will examine each sales representative efficiency for the last semester :
. Orders/Visits x 100
. Turnover/Orders
. Turnover/Visits
. Km/Visits
. Discounts/Turnover x 100

	Bob	Albert	John
Number of years in the company	3 years	10 years	6 months
Selling experience	4 years	5 years	1 year
Number of visits per semester	180	190	215
Number of orders per semester	65	100	60
Turnover per semester	€ 62,500	€ 125,000	€ 61,500
Time per visit	20 mn	30 mn	45 mn
Km per semester	1,600	1,000	1,320
% of prospection	10	5	35
Discounts amount	€ 6,250	€ 6,500	€ 2,850

Answers

T.V + - Paris

		Bob	Albert	John
Orders / Visits	65/180	36.1%	52.6%	27.9%
Turnover / Orders	62,500/65	961.54	1,250	1,025
Turnover / Visits	62,500/180	347.22	657.89	286.05
Km / Visits	1,600/180	8.89	5.26	6.13
Discounts / Turnover	6,250/62,500	10%	5.2%	4.6%

Albert is the best representative, it would be interesting to increase his commissions and bonuses.

Bob needs to be motivated with a training program and could make visits with Albert.

John is relatively efficient according to his short experience, he might have higher commissions.

Cheaper Jet – Roissy CDG

Managing the Cheaper Jet subsidiary in France, you have to motivate a new sales team aimed at business customers. The current pay system is based on a fixed wage (€ 1,000) and a commission on turnover (2 %).
The new pay system would include :
. a reduced fixed wage (€ 610),
. a commission on margin (9,5 %),
. individual sales objectives with special bonuses.
The sales objectives would increase by 5 % according to each monthly previous year turnover.
If the current year turnover equals the objective (100 % to 101 %), the bonus amounts to € 122.
If the current year turnover is above the objective (more than 101 %), an added bonus amounting to 10 % of the surplus will be distributed.
What would be the total pay of Brad TIP (current and new pay systems) according to his sales figures - comment the

	January	February	March	April
Current year turnover	55,950	45,580	68,900	64,500
Current year margin	16,230	11,360	20,670	16,120
Previous year turnover	54,880	44,210	64,490	60,980
Previous year margin	16,460	12,380	18,700	16,460

results :

1/ Previous pay system :

	January	February	March	April	Total
Fixed wage					
Commission					
Total Pay					

2/ New pay system :

	January	February	March	April	Total
Fixed wage					
Commission					
Objective					
Achievement rate (monthly objective)					
Bonus					
Total Pay					

Answers

Cheaper Jet – Roissy CDG

1/ Previous pay system :

	January	February	March	April	Total
Fixed wage	1,000	1,000	1,000	1,000	
Commission	1,119	911.6	1,378	1,290	
Total Pay	2,119	1,911.6	2,378	2,290	8,698.6

$1,119 = 55,950 \times 2\%$

2/ New pay system :

	January	February	March	April	Total
Fixed wage	610	610	610	610	
Commission	1541.85	1,079.2	1,963.65	1,531.4	
Objective	57,624	46,420.5	67,714.5	64,029	
Achievement rate (monthly objective)	97.09%	98.19%	101.75%	100.74%	
Bonus	-	-	240.55	122	
Total Pay	2,151.85	1,689.2	2,814.2	2,263.4	8,918.65

$240.55 = 122 + ((68,900 - 67,714.5) \times 10\% = 122 + 118.55$

Business Bank – Westford (U.S.A)

As a new manager of Business Bank– Westford (MA), you have to assess the retail bank figures and especially the mortgage loans turnover. Last year, the mortgage turnover reached by the sales team amounted to €k 3,642.86. The new objective for next year will increase by 12 %.

Mortgage turnover (€k) :

	January	February	March	April
Seasonal coefficient	0.6	0.8	1	1.2
Monthly mortgage turnover	257	317.56	328.32	335

1/ What will be the monthly mortgage objectives for next year – fill in the table below,

	January	February	March	April
Seasonal coefficient				
Monthly mortgage objective				
Cumulative objective				
Monthly mortgage turnover				
Cumulative turnover				
Variation : turnover minus objective				

Achievement rate : monthly objective				
Achievement rate : added objective				
Achievement rate : annual objective				

Comment the results.

2/ According to the figures in the table below, compare our Bank performance to the local Competitors – fill in the following table.

	Number of employees	Number of customers	Number of mortgage loans	Mortgage amounts (€k)	Competition performance
Our Bank	28.25	14,468	3,580	43,693	Active
Bank A	6	3,454	961	12,585	Weak
Bank B	12	6,500	1,429	17,407	Very active
Bank C	8	5,470	1,052	12,757	Weak
Bank D	11.75	5,540	1,312	22,444	Very active

Number of employees = Part time and Full time employees

.Local standards :

- number of customers per employee = 526
- number of mortgage loans per employee = 127
- mortgage amounts per employee (€k) = 1,859

	Number of employees	Customers per employee	Rank	Compared to the standard	Mortgages per employee	Rank	Compared to the standard
Our Bank							
Bank A							
Bank B							
Bank C							
Bank D							

(€k)	Amounts per employee	Rank	Compared to the standard
Our Bank			
Bank A			
Bank B			
Bank C			
Bank D			

Answers

Business Bank – Westford (U.S.A)

	January	February	March	April
Seasonal coefficient	0.6	0.8	1	1.2
Monthly mortgage objective (€k)	204	272	340	408
Cumulative objective	204	476	816	1224
Monthly mortgage turnover	257	317.56	328.32	335
Cumulative turnover	257	574.56	902.88	1237.88
Variation : turnover minus objective	53	45.56	-11.68	-73
Achievement rate : monthly objective	126%	117%	97%	82%
Achievement rate : added objective	126%	121%	111%	101%
Achievement rate : annual objective	6.3%	14.08%	22.13%	30.34%

€k = € 1,000 ; 3642.86 x 1.12 = 4,080 ;

In January : 4,080 x 0.6 / 12 months = €k 204 ;

53 = 257 – 204 ; 126% = 257 / 204 x 100 ;

6.3% = 257 / 4,080 x 100 ;

476 = 272 + 204 ; 574.56 = 317.56 + 257 ;

121% = 574.56 / 476 x 100 ; 14.08% = 574.56 / 4,080 x 100 ;

In March and April, sales slowdown. We should increase employees motivation by a sales contest with special gifts (purchase coupons or travel boxes).

	Number of employees	Customers per employee	Rank	Compared to the standard	Mortgages per employee	Rank	Compared to the standard
Our Bank	28.25	512.14	4	-	126.73	3	-
Bank A	6	575.67	2	+	160.17	1	+
Bank B	12	541.67	3	+	119.08	4	-
Bank C	8	683.75	1	+	131.5	2	+
Bank D	11.75	471.49	5	-	111.66	5	-

(€k)	Amounts per employee	Rank	Compared to the standard
Our Bank	1,546.65	4	-
Bank A	2,097.5	1	+
Bank B	1,450.58	5	-
Bank C	1,594.63	3	-
Bank D	1,910.13	2	+

512.14 = 14,468 / 28.25 ; 126.73 = 3,580 / 28.25 ;
1,546.65 = 43,693 / 28.25

Compared to the competition, our Bank results are disappointing. We should conquer new customers with local advertising and local events with real estate agents and notaries.

ComputerLand – New-York

You have been hired by the ComputerLand store in New York city. You must manage a sales team whom main target is small and middle size companies. The four sales executives use their own car for visiting their customers and prospects. They are paid back $ 2 per mile.

Hereafter their average yearly mileage :
. Mr A :   10,000 miles
. Mr B :   30,000 miles
. Mr C :   80,000 miles
. Mr D :   60,000 miles

In order to reduce these costs, you are studying two new options : car rental and car purchase :

1/ Car Rental costs for a S.U.V (sport and utility vehicle)
   . Yearly rental : $ 30,000
   . Insurance : $ 5,000
   . Cost per mile : $ 0.5

2/ Car purchase :
. SUV price : $ 70,000 (fully equipped with internet and office tools)
   . Depreciation : over 5 years,
   . Insurance : $ 4,000
   . Cost per mile :
$ 0.5 from 0 to 10,000 miles per year
$ 0.6 from 10,000 to 25,000 miles per year
$ 0.7 from 25,000 to 50,000 miles per year
$ 0.75 beyond 50,000 miles per year.

Which is the cheapest option for each sales executive and for the whole sales team ?

. Fill in the table below :

	Mr A	Mr B	Mr C	Mr D	Total
Present cost :					
Car rental :					
.rental cost					
.insurance					
.cost per mile					
Total :					
Car purchase :					
.depreciation					
.insurance					
.cost per mile					
Total :					

Option selected :

Answers

ComputerLand – New-York

	Mr A	Mr B	Mr C	Mr D	Total
Present cost :	20,000	60,000	160,000	120,000	360,000
Car rental :					
.rental cost	30,000	30,000	30,000	30,000	
.insurance	5,000	5,000	5,000	5,000	
.cost per mile	5,000	15,000	40,000	30,000	
Total :	40,000	50,000	75,000	65,000	230,000
Car purchase :					
.depreciation	14,000	14,000	14,000	14,000	
.insurance	4,000	4,000	4,000	4,000	
.cost per mile	5,000	21,000	60,000	45,000	
Total :	23,000	39,000	78,000	63,000	203,000

Option selected :
Mr. A (1), Mr. B (3), Mr. C (2), Mr. D (3), Team (3).

$20,000 = 10,000 \times 2$; $14,000 = 70,000 / 5$

CopyPro - Paris

Current pay system of the salespeople :

- Fixed wage : € 500 per month during 12 months,
- Commissions : 3 % of the turnover if the objective is achieved, 5 %, beyond the objective,
- Bonus : € 3,000 if the objective is achieved.
- Transportation costs are paid back : € 200 per month during 11 months,
- Social costs : € 400 per month during 12 months.
- The cost of the salesteam must equal or be under 15 % of the yearly turnover.

1/ What should be the minimum turnover of CopyPro sales team (5 salespeople) in order
to reach the cost objective ?

2/ Eventually, the sales manager requests the following yearly objective per sales person : € 75,000.
What would be the total yearly earning of a sales person if the objective is reached (100 %), if the objective is exceeded (130 %) ?

Cost of the sales team
(if the objective is achieved)

	Per sales person	Per sales team
Fixed wage		
Transportation		
Bonus		
Social cost		
Total		

Yearly earning of a sales person

	Objective reached at 100 %	Objective exceeded at 130 %
Fixed wage		
Commissions till 100 %		
Commissions over 100 %		
Bonus		
Transportation		
Total		

Answers

CopyPro - Paris

Cost of the sales team

	Per sales person	Per sales team
Fixed wage	6,000	30,000
Transportation	2,200	11,000
Bonus	3,000	15,000
Social cost	4,800	24,000
Total		80,000

.If the objective is achieved ; 6,000 = 500 x 12 ;
2,200 = 200 x 11

Yearly earning of a sales person

	Objective reached at 100 %	Objective exceeded at 130 %
Fixed wage	6,000	6,000
Commissions till 100 %	2,250	2,250
Commissions over 100 %	-	1,125
Bonus	3,000	3,000
Transportation	2,200	2,200
Total	2,250 = 75,000 x 3%	14,575

1,125 = 22,500 x 5% ; 22,500 = 97,500 − 75,000
97,500 = 75,000 + 30%

X = Turnover ; Y = Cost of the sales team ; $Y = 80,000 + 0.03\,X$; $Y = 0.15\,X$;
$0.15\,X = 80,000 + 0.03\,X$;
$0.15\,X - 0.03\,X = 80,000$; $0.12\,X = 80,000$; $X = 666,666.66$.

If the turnover amounts to 666,666.66, the cost of the sales team will amount to 80,000 + (666,666.66 x 0.03) ;

80,000 + 19,999.99 = 100,000 (15% of the turnover).

Business Culture

(True or False)
- Colour of life in Europe, yellow may be a symbol of death in the desert countries in Africa :
- Advertising expenditures are 650 times higher in France than in Ivory Coast :
- A German farmer wished to export to France a weight loss product called "T. Gross" :
- In England, "Genius" is a candy bar for cats :
- In some European countries, cheese is eaten with strawberries :
- A box of four soaps would not be sold in Japan, number 4 is unlucky :
- Positive in Asia, the cat may be a negative symbol in Africa :

Did you know it ?
- <u>In which country (Japan or United States), these are beliefs, attitudes and behavior</u> :

. Group work
. Everybody is like us
. A shareholder is a priority
. Successes, victory, heroism
. Harmony, consensus, compromise
. Sense of belonging to the company
. The company creates jobs
. The company creates profit
. The individual is a member of an organization
. We are unique

- <u>Which country uses the following currencies</u> :

. Rand	Thailand
. Riyal	Mexico
. Yuan	Japan
. Forint	Israel
. Rupee	Vietnam
. Yen	South Korea
. Shequel	India
	South Africa
. Bath	Saudi Arabia
. Dong	China
. Peso	Hungary
. Won	

- <u>In Which cities can you use these airports</u> :

. CDG :
. JFK :
. La Guardia :
. Heathrow :
. Newark :
. Stansted :
. Gatwick :
. O'Hare :
. Mirabel :
. Schiphol :
. Logan :
. Bora Bora :
. Fiumicino :
. Fortworth :

- From Paris, how long does it take to fly to these cities :
    - .17 H25   Los Angeles
    - .25 H   Papeete
    - .10 H30   Vancouver
    - .27 H   Boston
    - .6 H52   Grenoble
    - .0 H50   Noumea

- To which countries do these Airlines belong :
.Aeroflot, Lufthansa, Federal Express, KLM, Varig, Olympic Airways,
. Iberia, Finnair, Qantas, Avianca, Emirates, Air Perhaps, Continental Airlines.

(True or False)
- In the United States, what is the number one cause of death :
- On average, how many hours per day does an American watch television :
- Which U.S. state is the sixth largest economy in the world :
- Leading cause of death worldwide :
- In which country can you find the largest European shopping center :
- In India and China, the birth rate amounts to 130 boys for 100 girls :
- In South Korea, at the third birth, the ratio is 190 boys for 100 girls :
- In India, for questions of inheritance (the son is the one who inherits), survival of the surname and the practice of dowry, abortion and the abandonment of baby girls may occur :

- To fight these customs, the Indian government would like to offer two bicycles to each family that keeps a baby girl :
- At current rates, 36 million Indians might never find wives :
- The South Koreans are sometimes bringing their wives from Vietnam :
- Chinese saying : "A stupid boy is better than a clever girl" :
- Indian saying : "Raising a daughter is like watering the neighbor's garden" :
- Canadian saying : "Woman is the Future of Mankind" :
- Korean saying : "A married daughter is like wasting water" :
- 400,000 Americans die each year from diseases linked to excess of weight :
- In American fast-food restaurants, salads are sometimes twice more expensive than hamburgers :

World Records

. The four largest countries in km2 :
. The two smallest countries in km2 :
. The four most populated countries :
. The least populated country :
. Country with the highest density per km2 per capita :
. Country with the lowest density per km2 per capita :
. Largest country in the American continent :
. Largest country in the Asian continent :
. Largest country in Africa :
. The most populated country in Africa :

Capital – Country ?

- Colombo   Burma
- Damascus   New Zealand
- Ankara   Nepal
- Kathmandu   Turkey
- Amman   Armenia
- Pyongyang   Bhutan
- Yerevan   Cameroon
- Thimphu   Niger
- Rangoon   Syria
- Wellington   Sri Lanka
- Yaounde   Jordan
- Niamey   North Korea

Answers

Business Culture

(True or False)

- Colour of life in Europe, yellow may be a symbol of death in the desert countries in Africa :
True
- Advertising expenditures are 650 times higher in France than in Ivory Coast : *True*
- A German farmer wished to export to France a weight loss product called "T. Gross" : *False*
- In England, "Genius" is a candy bar for cats : *False*
- In some European countries, cheese is eaten with strawberries : *False (USA)*
- A box of four soaps would not be sold in Japan, number 4 is unlucky : *True*
- Positive in Asia, the cat may be a negative symbol in Africa : *True*

(Did you know it ?)

- <u>In which country (Japan or United States), these are beliefs, attitudes or behavior</u> :

. Group work	Jp
. Everybody is like us	US
. A shareholder is a priority	US
. Successes, victory, heroism	US
. Harmony, consensus, compromise	Jp
. Sense of belonging to the company	Jp
. The company creates jobs	Jp
. The company creates profit	US
. The individual is a member of an organization	Jp
. We are unique	US

- <u>Which country uses the following currencies</u> :

Thailand	*(Bath)*
Mexico	*(Peso)*
Japan	*(Yen)*
Israel	*(Shequel)*
Vietnam	*(Dong)*
South Korea	*(Won)*
India	*(Rupee)*
South Africa	*(Rand)*
Saudi-Arabia	*(Riyal)*
China	*(Yuan)*
Hungary	*(Forint)*

- <u>In Which cities can you use these airports</u> :

. CDG :	*Paris*
. JFK :	*New York*
. La Guardia :	*New York*
. Heathrow :	*London*
. Newark :	*New York*
. Stansted :	*London*
. Gatwick :	*London*
. O'Hare :	*Chicago*
. Mirabel :	*Montreal*
. Schiphol :	*Amsterdam*
. Logan :	*Boston*
. Bora Bora :	*Papeete*
. Fiumicino :	*Roma*
. Fortworth :	*Dallas*

- <u>From Paris, how long does it take to fly to these cities</u> :

.17 H25	Los Angeles *(10h30)*
.25 H	Papeete *(25h)*
.10 H30	Vancouver *(17h25)*
.27 H	Boston *(6h52)*
.6 H52	Grenoble *(0h50)*
.0 H50	Noumea *(27h)*

- <u>To which countries do these Airlines belong</u> :

. Aeroflot *Russia*, Lufthansa *Germany*, Federal Express *USA*, KLM *France*, Varig *Brésil*, Olympic Airways *Grèce*.

. Iberia *U.K*, Finnair *Finland*, Qantas *Australia*, Avianca *Colombia*, Emirates *UAE*, Air Perhaps, Continental Airlines *USA*.

- In the United States, what is the number one cause of death : *Obesity*
- On average, how many hours per day does an American watch television : *5 hours per day*
- Which U.S. state is the sixth largest economy in the world : *California*
- Leading cause of death worldwide : *Cancer*
- In which country can you find the largest European shopping center : *France, Paris.*
- In India and China, the birth rate amounts to 130 boys for 100 girls : *True*
- In South Korea, at the third birth, the ratio is 190 boys for 100 girls : *True*
- In India, for questions of inheritance (the son is the one who inherits), survival of the surname and the practice of

dowry, abortion and the abandonment of baby girls may occur :
True

- To fight these customs, the Indian government would like to offer two bicycles to each family that keeps a baby girl : *False*

- At current rates, 36 million Indians might never find wives : *True*

- The South Koreans are sometimes bringing their wives from Vietnam : *True*

- Chinese saying : "A stupid boy is better than a clever girl" : *True*

- Indian saying : "Raising a daughter is like watering the neighbor's garden" : *True*

- Canadian saying : "Woman is the Future of Mankind" : *False*

- Korean saying : "A married daughter is like wasting water" : *True*

- 400,000 Americans die each year from diseases linked to excess of weight : *True*

- In American fast food restaurants, salads are sometimes twice more expensive than hamburgers : *True*

World Records :

- The four largest countries in km2 :
Russia, Canada, China, Brazil
- The two smallest countries in km2 : *The Vatican, Monaco*
- The four most populated countries :
China, India, USA, Indonesia
- The least populated country :
The Vatican (860 inhabitants)
- Country with the highest density per km2 per capita :
Monaco
- Country with the lowest density per km2 per capita :
Mongolia
- Largest country in the American continent : *Canada*
- Largest country in the Asian continent : *China*
- Largest country in Africa : *Algeria*
- The most populated country in Africa : *Nigeria*

Capital – Country ?

. Colombo	*Sri lanka*
. Damascus	*Syria*
. Ankara	*Turkey*
. Kathmandu	*Nepal*
. Amman	*Jordan*
. Pyongyang	*North Korea*
. Yerevan	*Armenia*
. Thimphu	*Bhutan*
. Rangoon	*Burma*
. Wellington	*New Zealand*
. Yaounde	*Cameroon*
. Niamey	Niger

International Negotiation
(True - False)

- To have a monochronic behavior means that time is considered linear - you do only one thing at a time - the communication is direct, organized and detailed :
- The Scandinavians are more monochronic :
- The Mediterranean countries are monochronic :
- Spain and Italy often have a polychronic behavior – time is multidimensional :
- The notion of uncertainty varies between countries, Asian countries are rather fatalistic, Westerners are more anxious about an uncertain future :
- At a first business contact, the Swedes use the first name
- In South America, only leaders have the power to negotiate :
- In Japan, you have to remove your shoes in public places, especially in a supermarket :
- In Japan, for a business relationship, you do not shake hands and you avoid to be too close to your customer :
- In the United States, it is common to offer gifts to loyal customers :
- In Asia, business gifts are common and recommended :
- In Sweden, the meetings always start late :
- In Mexico or Saudi Arabia, to arrive on time seems very surprising :
- In the UK, a verbal agreement is very common :

Which negotiator is used to these behavior and attitudes :

. French Negotiatior – English Negotiator – Spanish Negotiator – German Negotiator :

- Clear and strong, few concessions, no relationship of friendship, only the result counts, logical presentation, structured, supported by figures, facts and references :

- Sense of pride and honor, modesty more than assertiveness, adept at haggling, interpersonal relationship appreciated, few group works :

- Reserve and self control, not expressing emotions, discretion on the personal and private life, taste for humor and self-deprecation, predominance of the oral over the written, a follower of customary law :

- Written documents are a priority with polite and complex expressions, ignorance of foreign languages, indirect communication, often intransigent, follower of the debates and arguments :

Answers

International Negotiation
(True - False)

- To have a monochronic behavior means that time is considered linear - you do only one thing at a time - the communication is direct, organized and detailed : *True*
- The Scandinavians are more monochronic : *True*
- The Mediterranean countries are monochronic : *False*
- Spain and Italy often have a polychronic behavior – time is multidimensional : *True*
- The notion of uncertainty varies between countries - Asian countries are rather fatalistic, Westerners are more anxious about an uncertain future : *True*
- At a first business contact, the Swedes use the first name : *True*
- In South America, only leaders have the power to negotiate : *True*
- In Japan, you have to remove your shoes in public places, especially in a supermarket : *False*
- In Japan, for a business relationship, you do not shake hands and you avoid to be too close to your customer : *True*
- In the United States, it is common to offer gifts to loyal customers : *True*
- In Asia, business gifts are common and recommended : *False*
- In Sweden, the meetings always start late : *False*
- In Mexico or Saudi Arabia, to arrive on time seems very surprising : True
- In the UK, a verbal agreement is very common : *True*.

Which negotiator is used to these behavior and attitudes :

. French Negotiatior – English Negotiator – Spanish Negotiator – German Negotiator :

- Clear and strong, few concessions, no relationship of friendship, only the result counts, logical presentation, structured, supported by figures, facts and references : *German*

- Sense of pride and honor, modesty more than assertiveness, adept at haggling, interpersonal relationship appreciated, few group works : *Spanish*

- Reserve and self control, not expressing emotions, discretion on the personal and private life, taste for humor and self-deprecation, predominance of the oral over the written, a follower of customary law : *English*

- Written documents are a priority with polite and complex expressions, ignorance of foreign languages, indirect communication, often intransigent, follower of the debates and arguments : *French*.

Great-Britain
(True or False)

- With record rainfalls in Europe, England is the number one country for convertible cars :
- The British often explain that God created in a lyric moment the most beautiful country in the world : France. Then, for the sake of balance, he created the French people :
- During World War II, the roof of a grocery store in London was hit by a German V1 missile.
The next day, the grocer posted up this panel "More open than ever " :
- A famous sentence of a European philosopher : "Continentals think life is a game, the British think that cricket is a game ! " :
- Every year the international championships of snail race take place in Birmingham :
- In the subway in London, the red seats are reserved for the British and blue folding seats to tourists :
- The famous red double-decker bus will be replaced by a three floor tram :
- During the "tea time", you must always pour the milk before tea :
- You never dip your toast in your tea mug :
- To flavor their tea, the English often add wine or whiskey :
- English women hold the European record of alcohol consumption :

International Communication
(Did you know it ?)

- In the United States, among 560 commercials that an American consumer may watch each day, how many are memorized : 2 - 72 - 9 - None.

- According to a survey of the American advertising market, which percentage of advertising budgets is spent in vain : 40% - 20% - 98%.

- Who said "I know that 50 % of my advertising budget is useless but the problem is that I do not know which one" : Henry Ford - Louis Renault – Steve Jobs.

- An Austrian store selling clothes in winter promised to offer a voucher of 370 euros to the first 5 customers who would come naked.
How many naked customers came : 2000 - 2 - None - 70.

- A famous doctrine of international marketing is :
  . "Think global, act local",
  . "Think local, act global"
  . "Think local, act local".

- Which is the world's largest exporting country :

- Which is the most indebted country in the world :

- What is the percentage of French exports aimed at European countries :

- Which is the first customer and first supplier of France :

- Classify in decreasing order these customers of France : United States - Germany - Benelux - United Kingdom - Spain - Italy

- Classify these countries in decreasing order (% of world exports) : U.S.A - European Union – Japan.

Great-Britain
(True or False)

- With record rainfalls in Europe, England is the number one country for convertible cars : *True*
- The British often explain that God created in a lyric moment the most beautiful country in the world : France. Then, for the sake of balance, he created the French people : *True*
- During World War II, the roof of a grocery store in London was hit by a German V1 missile.
The next day, the grocer posted up this panel "More open than ever " : *True*
- A famous sentence of a European philosopher : "Continentals think life is a game, the British think that cricket is a game ! " : *True*
- Every year the international championships of snail race take place in Birmingham : *False*
- In the subway in London, the red seats are reserved for the British and blue folding seats to tourists : *False*
- The famous red double-decker bus will be replaced by a three floor tram : *False*
- During the "tea time", you must always pour the milk before tea : *True*
- You never dip your toast in your tea mug : *True*
- To flavor their tea, the English often add wine or whiskey : *False*
- English women hold the European record of alcohol consumption : *True*

International Communication
(Did you know it ?)

- In the United States, among 560 commercials that an American consumer may watch each day, how many are memorized : 2 - 72 - 9 – None : *2*
- According to a survey of the American advertising market, which percentage of advertising budgets is spent in vain : 40% - 20% - 98% : *98%*
- Who said "I know that 50 % of my advertising budget is useless but the problem is that I do not know which one" : Henry Ford - Louis Renault – Steve Jobs : *Henry Ford*
- An Austrian store selling clothes in winter promised to offer a voucher of 370 euros to the first 5 customers who would come naked.

How many naked customers came : 2000 - 2 - None – 70 : *70*

- A famous doctrine of international marketing is :
  . "Think global, act local",
  . "Think local, act global"
  . "Think local, act local" : *Think global, act local.*
- Which is the world's largest exporting country : *Germany (in turnover), in volume (China).*
- Which is the most indebted country in the world : *USA*
- What is the percentage of French exports aimed at European countries : *80%*
- Which is the first customer and first supplier of France : *Germany*

- Classify in decreasing order these customers of France :

United States 6 – Germany 1 – Benelux 5 - United Kingdom 4 - Spain 2 – Italy 3.

- Classify these countries in decreasing order (% of world exports) :

U.S.A 2 - European Union 1 – Japan 3

- Case Studies -

The following case studies can be prepared in teams. We recommend a maximum of four students in the same team. The final mark can be dispatched between the oral presentation and the final document sent to the teacher.

Most of the informations regarding the studied company can be found on the internet, on companies web sites and in business books.

The main job of the different teams is to be able to present correctly the answers with an oral presentation and to prepare an interesting written document.

A computer and the usual software are necessary for these presentations.

Most of the case studies propose to create new advertising documents or videos.

Many students like these case studies because they find a mix of strategy and creation.

A/ With the help of the internet and their web site, please answer the following questions regarding « **International Airline** » :
(The teacher is free to choose a famous and real international airline)

1/ How could you explain the tremendous growth and Marketing success of
« **International Airline** » over the past few years ?

2/ What are the Pros and Cons of their Marketing Strategy ?

3/ How do the main International Airlines face this fierce competition ?

4/ How could you improve « **International Airline** » customer service for Premium passengers (propose and detail at least 3 new services) ?

5/ Prepare a 1 minute video commercial promoting « **International Airline** » in Europe, including a special offer for young travelers.

B/ « **Amusement Park** » :

1/ Analyse the marketing strategy of this Amusement Park with the help of a Swot matrix and the 5 Porter Forces chart (look for more informations on the internet and the park website).

2/ In order to attend the « Foire de Paris » next May, you have to create a 3D booth model promoting the park (maximum : 24 cm width, 26 cm height, 22 cm length) –

use paper, cardbox and any other material or your computer.

3/ With a view to convincing young customers in the Paris area, an advertising mail will be sent to 500,000 children – prepare this document including a contest and discount prices.

4/ A TV commercial will be broadcasted on T.V channels prepare this 4 mn infomercial for the « Amusement Park ».

C/ « **Video Report** » :

In order to study Services Marketing techniques used by French services companies, you have to prepare a **Video Report** in a service firm or store of your own choice (i.e : advertising agency, rental company, bank, hotel…)

You can prepare one or several interviews in english of different Managers and
Managing Directors regarding their Marketing methods.

After the video presentation, you will summarize and analyse the Marketing
Methods you would have observed.

D/ **Management** Case Studies :

With the help of the internet and their web site, please answer the following questions regarding « **XY Airways** » :

1/ What are « **XY Airways** » Management methods for improving customer service ?

2/ What do you think of their Management principles (detail the Pros and Cons in a table) ?

3/ In your opinion, could « **XY Airways** » Management system be used in a French Airline and how could you implement their methods ?

4/ Prepare a 1 minute « Facebook » video commercial promoting « **XY Airways** » management methods in order to recruit new employees in Europe.

E/ « **Computer Ltd** » :

1 / How can you explain the tremendous success of the **Computer Ltd** products and services all over the world ?

2/ What are the links between the marketing success of **Computer Ltd** and the Management methods of the company ?

3/ Please describe the main differences between « Previous CEO » Management methods and « New CEO » organisational techniques.

4/ Prepare a 5 mn video commercial promoting « **Computer Ltd** » in order to present to newly recruited executives the Management philosophy of the company.

From the same author

La Vie Epatante de l'Agent Secret Duchemin – Tome 1
Il Faut Sauver l'Agent Secret Duchemin – Tome 2
Agent Secret Duchemin – Mission Lune – Tome 3
Au Temps en Emporte l'Agent Duchemin – Tome 4
Le Fabuleux Destin de l'Agent Duchemin – Tome 5
Agent Secret Duchemin – En Avant Mars – Tome 6
Agent Secret Duchemin – A Mars Forcée – Tome 7

L'Effarante Aventure de Brian Tabernak – Tome 1
L'Incroyable Attaque de l'Agent Tabernak – Tome 2
La Terrible Traque de l'Equipe Tabernak – Tome 3
L'Equipe Tabernak Contre-Attaque – Tome 4
Des Agents pas très Secrets – Opération Esturgeon
Des Agents pas très Secrets – Mission Caméléon

Constantin Dumoulin – Panique sous les Tropiques
Constantin Dumoulin – Branle-Bas de Combat aux USA
Constantin Dumoulin – Secret Fatal au Lac Baïkal

Robin Dubois – Sans Froid ni Loi
Robin Dubois – Espion malgré moi

The Exciting Life of Secret Agent Duchemin – Volume 1
The Amazing Adventure of Brian Tabernak – Volume 1
The Incredible Attack of Agent Tabernak – Volume 2

Quiz de Marketing – Tome 1
Quiz de Marketing – Tome
Quiz de Marketing International
Quiz de Management Commercial
Comment s'autopublier en une journée ?
Marketing Quiz

www.ingramcontent.com/pod-product-compliance
Lightning Source LLC
Chambersburg PA
CBHW070644220526
45466CB00001B/282